Daniela Silva de Lara
Mariana De L. Rivaben
Glaucineia Gomes de Lima

Psycho-oncology: Mother-daughter relationship

Daniela Silva de Lara
Mariana De L. Rivaben
Glaucineia Gomes de Lima

Psycho-oncology: Mother-daughter relationship

ScienciaScripts

Imprint

Any brand names and product names mentioned in this book are subject to trademark, brand or patent protection and are trademarks or registered trademarks of their respective holders. The use of brand names, product names, common names, trade names, product descriptions etc. even without a particular marking in this work is in no way to be construed to mean that such names may be regarded as unrestricted in respect of trademark and brand protection legislation and could thus be used by anyone.

Cover image: www.ingimage.com

This book is a translation from the original published under ISBN 978-3-330-99511-6.

Publisher:
Sciencia Scripts
is a trademark of
Dodo Books Indian Ocean Ltd. and OmniScriptum S.R.L publishing group

120 High Road, East Finchley, London, N2 9ED, United Kingdom
Str. Armeneasca 28/1, office 1, Chisinau MD-2012, Republic of Moldova, Europe
Printed at: see last page
ISBN: 978-620-8-17494-1

Daniela Silva de Lara
Glaucineia Gomes de Lima
Mariana De Luccia Rivaben

PSYCHO-ONCOLOGY: MOTHER-AUGHTER RELATIONSHIP

"If you look hard enough, everyone has a mole, a bladder mark or a vaccine. And there's chilblains, roundworms, amoebae, only the ballerina doesn't have them. And she doesn't have an itch, a rash or a chilblain, nor does she lack manners. If you look closely, everyone has lice, or smells of creolin. Everyone has a half-eyed brother, only the ballerina doesn't..." (Ciranda da Bailarina - Chico Buarque de Holanda).

SUMMARY

<u>**Summary**</u>

This paper discusses the mother-daughter relationship in the face of the onset of psycho-oncological illness, from a psychoanalytic perspective. In many cases, the child's suffering appears in somatic phenomena. Freud theorized that the psychic can influence physical processes, that is, the animic affects the physical. Through a theoretical-practical study, three girls aged between eight and ten with cancer were chosen and interviews with their mothers and observations of the children were carried out. We selected some data from the children's history and the onset of the disease and used excerpts from their speeches to illustrate the theoretical reflection. In the mothers' speeches, impasses emerged in relation to the place that the child occupied in their fantasies, before and after the illness, the denial of their daughters' illness and the difficulty in mourning the idealized image of the child constructed by the maternal fantasy. The child seems to evoke for the mother her lost childhood and the child's body can be a means of expressing the family's unease. When mothers learn of the diagnosis of a chronic and fatal illness, they sometimes seek refuge in denial of their child's illness, building a barrier between their fantasy (idealized child) and reality (sick child). The mourning of the idealized son, the bearer of all perfection, needs to be dealt with, so that the mother doesn't become paralyzed in her narcissistic wound and starts to help her daughter build her own narcissism, her body image and can see more than a sick son. We have seen in the cases explained that, rather than an event in the child's body, somatic illness is a fact of discourse, which is linked to the place that the child occupies in the parental fantasy. The conclusion is that, in addition to organic suffering, it is also necessary to locate the discourse of the sufferer and the adults who care for the sick child, as well as the infantile and maternal fantasies in relation to getting sick.

Key words: mother-daughter relationship, psycho-oncology and psychoanalysis.

Introduction

I had been interested in doing research into childhood cancer since before I was at university. It was based on a strong interest in working in the health sector. The growing number of cases of children with oncological illnesses increased interest and the decision was made to understand the onset of the disease in relation to the family context.

Contact with Freud's theories aroused our curiosity to understand the complexity of the mother-daughter relationship, and we chose to discuss the mother-daughter relationship in the emergence of oncological diseases.

This study aims to understand the mother-child relationship in the face of psycho-oncological illnesses and to discuss and reflect on the importance of this relationship in the face of oncological illnesses. It also aims to assess the rate at which this type of illness occurs in children.

The nature of the study is theoretical and practical, with field research consisting of interviews with mothers and the observation of three girls with oncological diseases and the collection of data on the history of these children, which allows us to relate the position of the disease in relation to the child and their position in the family structure.

The general aim of this work is to discuss the importance of the mother-girl relationship in psychosomatic illness, specifically in the appearance of oncological diseases in girls, from a psychoanalytic perspective.

We surveyed the psychoanalytic literature on psychosomatic illness and, through this reference, we discussed the importance of the mother-girl relationship, as well as differentiating the medical and psychoanalytic views on somatic illness.

The theoretical study, the observation of female children and the analysis of their conversations (mothers and children) were carried out in an institution that cares for children with oncological diseases. Three cases of girls with cancer were selected. Interviews were conducted with the mothers to gather data on the child's history and also on the onset of the disease. The mother was informed that the data would be used for research and signed an informed consent form.

The interview was semi-directed, with the central focus on the mother-daughter relationship in the face of cancer, where care was taken not to touch on issues that mobilized a lot of anguish or made the mother feel guilty about her daughter's illness. The mother spoke about her daughter and, based on her speech, issues such as: data relating to the birth, the onset of the illness and the effects of the illness on the relationship between mother and daughter were privileged. The analysis of excerpts from the selected speeches served to illustrate the theoretical discussion.

Working in hospitals has proved to be an open field for psychology professionals; in general or pediatric hospitals, work in the children's area has emerged as a field of activity for psychologists. For psychology, this new area allows professionals to question the scope of their work in medicine and other areas of health, which contributes to an interlocution between professionals from both areas. This makes it possible to re-dimension the issue of illness, based on an understanding of the relationships that are established around it.

The first chapter discusses the mother-child relationship, emphasizing the importance of the Oedipus complex, especially in the case of the girl, who at first falls in love with her mother and then transfers this love to her father, a transfer that also occurs with her erogenous zone, moving from the clitoris to the vagina. The girl has her mother as her first love object and this love will leave its mark on the child's subjectivity.

In the second chapter, psychoanalysis applied to childhood is a process that involves not only the child, but also their parents. The development of a symptom is greatly influenced by the mother-child relationship, and this is revealed through the speeches, where the relationship with the mother is evident.

The third chapter deals with psychosomatic illness, in which the relationship between the physical and the animic is reciprocal, the affective state leads to impairments in the physical, and individual experiences influence the meaning of the symptom.

The chapter Psycho-oncology and childhood cancer presents the importance of psychological support for people with oncological diseases. This area is under development by health professionals. Childhood cancer is rare, affects cells of the blood system and most often occurs as a result of genetic predisposition. Most children who are diagnosed early and treated in specialized centers have a high chance of being cured.

This work aims to contribute to the training of students by highlighting the importance of discussing children with psychosomatic illness from a psychoanalytic perspective. It is hoped that understanding the influence of the mother-child relationship on psychosomatic illness will lead to a reflection on the relationship between the body and the psyche, an important discussion for psychology.

Next, the analysis of the mothers' statements and the observation of the children will be presented, in an attempt to articulate them with the theoretical framework. This work hopes to contribute by highlighting the importance of the mother-daughter relationship and its influence on the emergence of oncological diseases.

Theoretical Reference

1. Mother-Child Relationship

Freud (1909 [1908]) states that, for children, parents are seen as the ultimate authority and source of knowledge; when they are little, they want to be like their parents, girls like their mothers and boys like their fathers. As children develop, they get to know their friends' parents and, comparing them with their own, they evaluate them and may question the previously incomparable qualities they attributed to them. They then begin to criticize their parents for preferring characteristics that others have.

The child is extremely attached to the parent of the opposite sex, while his bond with the other parent is hostile; the boy bonds with his mother and the father becomes his rival; the girl, on the other hand, initially establishes an intense and loving relationship with her mother, because in both cases she satisfies the child's vital needs, which she then transfers to the father. The father had previously been her rival, but this doesn't even compare to the rivalry he faces with the boys. The mother is now seen with hatred, a feeling that can persist all her life, or can be overcompensated; part of it is overcome and part is persistent (Freud, 1932).

In Freud's (1932) understanding, after exchanging her original object (the mother for the father), the girl has the complicated task of transferring her main genital area, the clitoris, which originally constituted her, to a new one. She used to live in a masculine way, getting pleasure from the excitement of the clitoris while keeping her desires focused on her mother. Because she envied the penis, she lost the pleasure she felt, discovered she was castrated, repudiated her love for her mother and transferred her genital area to the vagina, which is specifically female. The man, on the other hand, only needs to continue with the activity he has always carried out, maintaining his original erogenous zone.

The girl then turns to her father in search of the penis that her mother denied her. However, this desire is only really fulfilled when it is replaced by the desire to have a baby. However, this desire had occurred before and had gone unnoticed. In the phallic phase, when she played with dolls, this toy was not in fact an expression of her femininity but an attempt to become self-sufficient, replacing her passivity in relation to her mother (she tries to do with the toy what her mother usually does with her).

The girl attributes the castration to herself. Gradually, she extends it to other women and, finally, to her mother. For this reason, she begins to distance herself from her mother, and this gradually happens.

According to Freud (1931), we had to take into account the possibility that a certain number of women remained stuck in their original bond with their mothers and never achieved a real change towards men. At that time, due importance was given to the pre-oedipal phase in women.

When a woman discovers that she has been castrated, she attributes this to male superiority and rebels against this undesirable state. From this, divided, three lines of development open up, which are, firstly, denial, secondly, confrontation and, finally, elaboration.

For Freud (1931, p.174):

> The girl, frightened by the comparison with boys, grows dissatisfied with her clitoris, abandons her phallic activity and, with it, her sexuality in general, as well as much of her masculinity in other fields. The second line leads her to cling with defiant self-affirmation to her threatened masculinity. Until an unbelievably late age, he clings to the hope of getting a penis at some point. This hope becomes the goal of their life and the fantasy of being a man, despite everything, often persists as a formative factor for long periods. This masculinity complex in women can also result in a manifest homosexual object choice. Only if her development follows the third, very indirect path, will she reach the final normal feminine attitude, in which she takes the father as her object, thus finding her way to the form of the Oedipus complex.

When women choose a husband to model themselves after their father, they end up repeating with him, in their married life, the bad relationship they had with their mother. This is explained by regression. The woman's relationship with her mother was the original (first), and her bond with her father was built on it; in marriage, the original relationship emerges from repression (Freud, 1932).

In addition to castration, there are other factors that make the girl move away from her mother: jealousy of other people (siblings, rivals and even her father), childish love, because *"the demands of a child's love are unlimited; they demand exclusivity and do not tolerate sharing"* (Freud, 1932, p. 152), and the fact that the mother awakens sexual activity and later forbids *it*.

The child sometimes feels neglected and regrets having to share their parents' love with their siblings; they have the feeling that their affection is not reciprocated, so they imagine they are adopted; or that their parents are actually their stepfather and stepmother. Boys have greater impulses to feel their father's hostility and a desire to be free of it; girls no longer show this feeling so strongly. Later, in the phase that Freud (1909 [1908]) calls the neurotic's family romance, the child's imagination is focused on replacing their parents with others who have a better social position, and at this stage the child is unaware of the sexual determinants of procreation. When the child learns about the roles played by the parents in their sexual relationships, the family romance is then content to exalt the role of the father, while the mother is quite right, and no longer questions the maternal origin, but only the father.

"The child then tends to imagine itself in erotic relationships and situations, the motivating force of which is the desire to place the mother (the object of the most intense sexual curiosity) in situations of secret infidelity and secret love affairs" (Freud, 1909[1908], p.245). The fantasies, which were once asexual, are now known and a reason for revenge and retaliation, they are introjected by neurotic critics who have possibly been punished by their parents for sexual behavior.

When children want to replace their parents, they just want to remember past times when their father was a hero and their mother was the most beautiful of women. So she turns her back on her current father in order to return to the father she trusted in her early childhood years.

The girl's rivalry with her mother and her hostile behavior is in no way a consequence of the Oedipus complex, but originates in the preceding phase and is reinforced by the Oedipal situation.

The Oedipus complex is the central phenomenon of the sexual period of early childhood and its dissolution is followed by the latency period (Freud, 1924). The dissolution of the Oedipus complex occurs due to the unfulfillment of the child's desire, and this lack of success leads to the destruction of the Oedipus complex. The child's sexual development takes place up to the stage in which the genital organ takes on its main function. This happens with the penis, because the female genital organ has not yet been discovered.

The Oedipus complex in boys, like in girls, has a dual orientation (active and passive). The boy desires his father's love and wants to occupy his mother's role. In the beginning of the Oedipus complex, the boy has no rivalry with his mother and has a feeling of affection for his father.

Another characteristic of this phase is early childhood masturbation, the repression of which by parents gives rise to the fear of castration. Nocturnal enuresis and its suppression is seen as an inhibition of genital activity and originates from the threat of castration. A very young child who hears his parents copulating may have an early sexual development and this may also trigger his first sexual arousals.

Masturbation is not responsible for entering the phallic phase, but rather the discovery that girls will make that their brother's or classmate's penis is bigger than hers (clitoris), thus arousing envy. For the boy, this discovery doesn't make much difference at first, it doesn't interest him. Later, with the threat of castration, observation becomes important. This discovery also produces two feelings in the boy: horror at the mutilated creature, or contempt for it.

When the boy starts to manipulate his genitals, that's when he ends up directing his interest to that area of his body. He ends up discovering that his parents (or adults in general) don't approve of this behavior. Then comes the threat of castration, which is not directed at the penis, but at the active culprit of masturbation (the hand). When these threats start to appear to children, they generally don't believe that castration can occur. However, when the boy sees the female genital organ, he becomes convinced of the absence of a penis. Thus, the threat of castration takes effect. The Oedipus complex is dissolved by the threat of castration.

At this point, according to Freud (1924, p. 221):

Object cathexis is abandoned and replaced by identification. The authority of the father or parents is introjected into the ego and there forms the core of the superego, which assumes the father's severity and perpetuates the prohibition against incest, thus defending the ego from the return of libidinal cathexis. The libidinal tendencies belonging to the Oedipus complex are partly desexualized and sublimated (something that probably happens with every transformation into an identification) and partly inhibited in their objective and transformed into impulses of affection. The whole process, on the one hand, preserved the genital organ - removed the danger of its loss - and, on the other, paralyzed it - removed its function.

The girl is left with the desire to have a penis and so, faced with the incessant search, ends up behaving like a man, or just refuses to accept castration and believes she has a penis. However, after realizing this fact, she develops a feeling of inferiority.

Freud (1925, p. 315) states that: *"Even after penis envy has abandoned its true object, it continues to exist: by means of an easy displacement, it persists in the characteristic trait of jealousy".* Jealousy is part of the mental life of both sexes, but for women it *is* reinforced by displaced penis envy. Another consequence of penis envy *is* the girl's more distant bond with her mother.

In the girl, the clitoris *is* initially seen as the penis, and when the female sexual organ is compared to the male, the girl feels inferior and unjustified. For the girl, at some point in her life, she had a penis, but lost it due to castration. She doesn't understand the lack of a male organ as a characteristic of sex.

Masturbation is less tolerated by women, and the problem may lie in assimilating clitoral masturbation to male masturbation. Abandoning it brings women closer to developing femininity. This distancing between masturbation and the development of femininity is also due to the recognition of the difference between the genital organs.

Boys' Oedipus complex is resolved when they are faced with the threat of castration. Girls, on the other hand, are introduced into this phase due to the castration complex, as it encourages femininity, while castration for boys limits masculinity.

It's not just a repression of the Oedipus complex, it's literally destroyed, its objects are incorporated into the ego and form the core of the superego, thus ceasing to exist.

According to Freud (1925,p 319-320):

...for women, the level of what is ethically normal is different from what it is in men. The superego is never as inexorable, as impersonal, as independent of its emotional origins as we demand it to be in men. The character traits that we have criticized from all eras against women - who show less sense of justice than men, who are more often influenced in their judgments by feelings of affection or hostility - are all largely explained by the modification in the formation of their superego that we inferred above.

The child's sexuality is not limited to the choice of the beloved object; interest in the genitals takes on a dominant dimension during the development of sexuality. For both sexes, the child only considers the male genitalia, as this represents the phallus.

The boy realizes the distinction between men and women, but believes that everyone has the same genital organ, including inanimate abjects; only later does he realize that the penis is not common to everyone.

The girl at first believes she has a penis, which is small and still growing; later she thinks she had a penis, but that it was taken away by someone. The lack of a penis is seen as the result of castration and the child is faced with the task of coming to terms with castration in relation to itself (Freud, 1908).

The children thus believed that only women with some inadmissible feat were without penises. Later, when they turn to the origin of the birth of babies, they discover that only women are capable of giving birth to a child. At this point, they lose their penis; as if they had exchanged it for a baby. It is only at puberty that masculinity and femininity are defined, and the vagina is then conceived as a place to "store" the penis.

2. Psychoanalysis applied to children

Psychoanalysis applied to children is the same as that applied to adults. The analyst works in language and, even if the child doesn't speak, the discourse in this case is a collective discourse, encompassing: father, mother and child; which is constituted around the child's symptom (Mannoni, 1987).

The discourse is much more about lost dreams than reality (Mannoni, 1987). The child carries with them the mission of repairing their parents' frustrations and fulfilling their lost dreams. An analysis can even identify the mark of words spoken or not spoken on the somatic.

According to Mannoni (1987), a word constitutes the individual's truth, even when it is not real, and its formulation must be integrated into the discourse of the unconscious. Childhood memories become meaningful when they are situated in relation to desire. These discoveries lead us to the language of the unconscious.

Freud's research went in two directions: on the one hand, the meaning of the symptom, which he saw as an unspoken word, and on the other, his belief in the physiological. In adults, analysis aims to reach childhood memories, which is why child analysis was seen as inconceivable. It was only through medical-pedagogical perspectives that it gained momentum.

For Mannoni (1987, p. 21):

> The analyst is then confronted with his or her own representation of childhood and the weight of his or her unconscious motivations will be reflected in the orientation given to the cure; the child and his or her family challenge the analyst in his or her oldest fears, defenses and anguish - he or she is constantly brought to a level where everyone is confronted with the problem of desire, death and the law.

Freud (1933) shows the function of the superego in repressing incestuous impulses; the origin of certain children's fear of the ascendant of the same sex, a fear that is transformed into an internal threat and then projected outwards into the world perceived as dangerous. The difficulties encountered in child psychoanalysis are external, influenced by the relationship with the parents.

Parents play an important role, they have to recognize the child's individuality, intervene based on indications of what's going on in their child's mind, give them love, while maintaining authority.

The first years of childhood, according to Freud (1933[1932]), are of great importance because of the emergence of sexuality which has consequences for maturity and because the impressions of this phase occur in an immature ego, acting as traumas. By repressing the traumas, the ego becomes vulnerable to further illness and functional disorders. When he talks about the place of parents in childhood, he is less talking about their real qualities than about what also marked them in childhood.

For Mannoni (1987) the word fair is complicated to introduce because it takes the mother to her own reference point; if answers remain closed to the child, he will find it difficult to understand her question in any other way than through confusion.

In 1908, Freud spoke for the first time about play in children. He says that children create their own world by rearranging their ideas. Children's favorite pastime is playing. When they do this, they behave like a creative writer, creating their own world. Children take their play very seriously and put a lot of emotion into it. In children's play, there is a separation between the world of fantasy and the real world. Children like to play, linking their imagined objects and situations with reality, and it is this situation that differentiates children's play from fantasizing (daydreams). (Freud, 1908[1907]).

Children's play is pleasurable and it's where they project their fantasies and desires, as well as helping their development. They play with friends, alone, in front of adults or not. Whatever the situation, children don't hide their play or even feel ashamed, unlike adults. They expose their desire, their desire to be an adult, in play and have no reason to hide it.

Freud (1920) reports that children reproduce unpleasant events in play, by repeating what has been done to them. The game is then presented as something to decipher. For adults, expressing this desire is very difficult, because they are expected to act in the real world, and on the other hand, these desires have characteristics that it is essential to hide. Adults feel ashamed of their fantasies, which are mostly ambitious or erotic desires (Freud, 1908[1907]).

Fantasies are pleasurable and are expressed by adults through daydreams. What creates the daydream are the situations experienced by the subject. The present, past and future are united by desire. In their first years of life, children go through identity conflicts. Regardless of how the child views the world, there is no dual situation to structure the

Oedipus complex. Any intervention by an adult runs the risk of fixing the child in a regressive behavior, chosen to be in what they believe to be their mother's.

It is possible to find in the individual's history the mother's words linked to a bodily emotion in the child that affirms the trauma and keeps the discourse marked in order to hide the original text.

As long as the subject remains alienated in their symptom, the disorder appears at the level of the imaginary.

To the extent that the word becomes non-mystifying, it changes the individual's position vis-à-vis the other's desire; the problem of communication was addressed by Freud (1932) who emphasized the child's belief in the omnipotence of adult thoughts. There are analysts who believe that the transmission of thoughts occurs only between mother and child, making it clear that the child's unconscious is informed as far as the mother wishes or refuses. It is extremely important for analysts to consider the maternal word in the healing of the child.

Symptoms always involve the individual and the other, so they develop with an Other and for an Other. The hidden meaning is revealed in the symptoms.

The relationship with the mother is always present in children's speeches. When there is an organic illness in the child, the child faces not only this difficulty, but also the way in which the mother uses this illness in the phantasmatic world, which ends up being shared in the relationship.

Psychoanalysis seeks to highlight the real situation experienced by the child and their family, not underestimating the reality of the illness. The child values the discourse of his or her family members about the illness, and it is these words that create the child's experience. The psychoanalyst then seeks to understand the words condensed in the anguish of an illness, allowing the child to make sense of life.

Another important aspect is the way in which the child was expected, beyond the paternal projections, their real existence clashes with the unconscious projections, giving rise to misunderstandings. In some cases, the child may feel barred from a real word, looking to the illness as an opportunity to express themselves.

3. Psychosomatic illness

Psychic treatment, according to Freud (1904), means treatment that starts from the soul, whether it is composed of physical or animistic disturbances, acting first on what is animistic in the human being.

For Freud, the relationship between the physical and the animic is reciprocal; animic states are expressed by the physical; psychosomatic illness is an example. The affective state causes observable changes in the physical; an individual in a depressed state can show impairment in the body, being more vulnerable to the appearance of pathologies; conversely, in a state of happiness, the person has greater energy, disposition; which leaves them with a more youthful expression. The length of life is also related to depressive affections, which can shorten life, like sudden joy.

In his text "The Meaning of Symptoms" (1917 [1916]), the father of psychoanalysis states that the meaning of a physical symptom is related to the patient's experiences. The more singular the experiences, the greater the relationship between meaning and symptom.

The effect of each procedure dictated by the doctor is made up of two parts: respect for medicine and the patient's physical behavior. The miraculous cures, linked to faith, the placebo effect; are explained by the animic power.

Ever since doctors recognized the power of words, which are the most effective way to bring about transformations, they have been directing the patient's emotional state towards more appropriate paths, which is called emotional treatment. Medicine has been adding emotional components to the dynamics of some illnesses, referring its patients to specialists in this area.

Doctors have always practiced animistic treatment, especially in ancient times when nothing else was available except the psyche and the effect of pogoes.

According to Freud (1914, p. 93):

> A person tormented by pain and organic malaise is no longer interested in things in the external world, insofar as they don't concern their suffering. A closer look shows us that they also withdraw libidinal interest from their love objects: while they suffer, they stop loving. The banality of this fact doesn't mean that we

16

can't translate it in terms of libido theory. We should then say: the sick man withdraws his libidinal cathexis back into his own ego, and puts it out again when he recovers.

For psychoanalysis, there is a tendency towards conscious and unconscious disaggregation (dissociation of connections in the psychic field) in the psyche, as a result of which the unconscious process does not reach the conscious. Psychic life originates from the interaction of forces, which can inhibit or favor each other.

If a group of ideas remains in the unconscious, psychoanalysis doesn't interfere, because there is a capacity for synthesis, which is evident in this dissociation (conscious and unconscious), but it states that the unconsciousness and isolation of these ideas was caused by another group of ideas. This process is called repression.

Repression plays an extremely important role in psychic life, but there can be failures which are preconditions for the formation of symptoms. This is because these ideas are in opposition to other ideas and are therefore repressed.

It is important to emphasize that psychoanalysis has its theory based on the psychic, but psychoanalysts always keep in mind that the psychic and the organic are in constant interaction.

The link between the psychic and the organic gave rise to psychosomatics, which provides an approach to human illness, somatization in the body due to the influence of the psychic. In adopting the term somatize, it is used to express contempt for the complaint of the sufferer, rather than an explanation of the cause of the illness.

Freud was the pioneer of psychosomatics, when he reflected on the relationship between the psychic and the somatic. Other authors also made contributions, such as George Graddeck, Fdlix Deutch and Franz Alexander, who founded the Chicago School; they worked to apply psychoanalysis, developing a psychosomatic approach to organ pathology.

H. Selly, starting from physiology, in 1936 described the General Adaptation Syndrome, a set of physiological reactions that prepares the organism to defend itself against aggression, comprising three phases: alarm at the threat, resistance to the threat and exhaustion.

From the 1970s onwards, a new field of research was defined: Neuropsychoimmunology. The discovery of neurobiological networks reinforced the hypothesis that psychological factors play a role in the genesis of diseases such as cancer.

The work of researchers from the Institute of Psychosomatics in Paris continues to contribute to highlighting the involvement of psycho-emotional factors such as allergies, migraines, hypertension and cancer. The contributions focus on: the etiological dimension of the pathology, the child's early relationships with parents and the therapeutic environment.

Freud's theory has two models for understanding somatization: the hysterical conversation, characterized as a somatic conversation of psychic energy, with symptoms related to infantile sexual conflicts, and the current neurosis, characterized by anguish, a functional symptomatology, reactions to the impossibility of discharging present excitations.

There are three ways in which excitations are discharged: organically, motorically and through thought. If an individual has a deficient psychic structure, he or she may be prevented from reacting to a traumatic situation by dreams or psychic defense mechanisms, using organic pathways as the channel for discharging his or her excitations. All pathology is an attempt to establish balance in the organism, which cannot cope with the internal or external tensions it is subjected to.

The development of child psychosomatics has been going on since the 1970s, between pediatricians and psychoanalysts at the Institute of Psychosomatics in Paris. Among the pioneers were Michel Fain, Michel Soule, Leon Kreisler and Rosine Debray.

Rene Spitz was one of the first to study the primitive relationships between babies and the people in their environment, highlighting the importance of the mother-child relationship, describing three organizing points of the infant psyche: the smile as a response to the adult, the anguish in the face of the stranger and the "no".

Childhood disorders are then understood as failures in primitive relationships and in the maternal function; the baby discharges the excess excitement it is subjected to into the somatic, because it doesn't yet have psychic autonomy. Excitement, explained by Freud in Л1ёш of the pleasure principle; with the concept of the death drive, the excitement does not follow a fulfillment of desire, causing a state of tension in the psychic apparatus, retained in a closed and repetitive circuit, waiting for a moment to progress, the concept of the death drive.

The psychosomatic phenomenon is a dysfunction of the biological as a result of the processes experienced in the transition from the biological body to the drive order. The body suffers because it doesn't speak, and there is no obvious conflict that has a displaced or condensed expression in the symptom. The distraught child is looking for a guiding word, an understanding of what is happening to him. Not knowing the meaning, the child becomes frightened and thirsts for knowledge (of words) (Mannoni, 1987).

According to Mannoni (1987, p.32):

The word fair is not easy to introduce, because it leads the mother to her own system of references. If answers must remain closed to her, the child will find it difficult to introduce her question in any other way than through the disorder of her behavior.

The child is in constant search of the right word. They are ready to disqualify what has been said so that the truth can be given to them. Everything that is said to the child is assimilated by them in a concrete way and they take it as truth. The child's discourse is made up of what the adult can bear and it is through lies that the child responds to the adult's lie.

It is because of the absence of true meaning in language that the symptom manifests itself, saying what it has to say. Mannoni (1987) reports that the adult's words mark and cause subsequent changes in the child's personality. It's the words, or even the lack of them, that hurt the imagination.

The word in discourse comes as a mark. The symptom (phantom) appears as a smoke that hides the real problem. The individual remains alienated in his ghost and the disorder is felt in the imaginary. The symptom always involves the individual and the other.

What emerges then is not the true event, but the lie that the adults tell about it. The child is faced with a dilemma: tell the lie or mystify it. The symptom appears in the absence of a word, coming as a mask or an encrypted word. The child provides the mother with the word that deceives (the symptom) for her to decipher. She hides her knowledge from her mother, because she doesn't want to listen, passing on her knowledge in a coded way. Most of the time, the mythical story presented by the child brings the solution to the symptom, the cure. *"The symptom appears as a word by which the individual designates (in enigmatic form) the way in which he situates himself in the face of every relationship of desire"*. (Mannoni, 1987, p.50-51).

In the situation of illness, the child's discourse gives us a glimpse of their relationship, of their mother's anguish. In this situation, the aim is to show how the real problem is experienced by the child and their family, looking for the meaning that individuals attribute to this situation. For the child, the words spoken, or even their omission by their family group, are what will matter and allow them to make sense of the events they are experiencing.

Psychoanalysis is an applied psychology for investigating the mind and is a therapeutic method. It is concerned with unconscious functions and aims at self-knowledge. Psychosomatic medicine studies the relationship between body and mind, emphasizing the psychological aspects of pathologies. Psychoanalysis has shown that the physical-bodily system is transformed into the human-psychological system, not nullifying any one system, but rather one opening the door to the other. Medicine sees man from his illness, only from a medical point of view. Psychosomatic medicine understands the patient's illness through the patient himself. This is the role of psycho-oncology (Schavelzon, 1999).

According to Eksterman (1992, p. 78):

> Several concepts converge to characterize this space where biological activities are transformed into mental ones. One of them is the transformation of the primary process into a secondary one, or, in other words, what is experienced as concrete, real, is transmuted into something abstract, virtual, capable of being conscious.

The body is created and recreated through mental representations. The influence of the mental process on somatic functions is what raises suspicions about the influence of the psychological on the somatic. The mind, when constructing its vision of the world, experiences its creations as real and projects them outwards to external reality. The body, in turn, adapts to this and transforms it into its reality.

Pediatric medicine is an area of medicine that monitors the growth and development of children, looking at both curative and preventive aspects. When we talk about child psychiatry and psychology, the vast majority of pediatricians disqualify them, which means that children's families don't worry about the psychological aspects of an illness, but only the somatic ones.

Parents then end up not dealing with this issue due to medical resistance to discussing it. Issues of mental and environmental hygiene end up becoming inappropriate and not belonging to medicine (Mello, 1992).

Treating a child doesn't simply mean eliminating the symptoms of a problem, it means taking care of the child as a whole, taking into account all the aspects that may be involved in their pathology, always with the spirit of prevention in mind.

For families, in psychological consultations they believe that psychosomatic disorders must have an organic origin, or they try to omit the organic symptomatology because they consider it a fatality.

Psychosomatic disorders in children require extensive research, not only with adults, but also in child psychiatry because of the value of the illness for children and their families. For medicine, the first intervention is extremely important for understanding the case and the sequence of events. The psychosomatic investigation of a child takes place between the child, the environment and the doctor. Somatic problems are a picture that needs to be looked at in two ways: organically and psychologically, with one symptom clarifying the other.

According to Kreisler (1999, p.316):

One of the central ideas of psychosomatics is based on the relationship between somatic balance and the quality of the affective foundations of the personality. In the primary phase, the defensive instincts, later guaranteed by the Ego, are supported by maternal management in the dual interaction.

Child psychosomatic clinical knowledge has its origins in pediatrics and psychoanalysis. In the study of psychosomatics, it is necessary to analyze these two aspects in order to obtain a global understanding of the condition. *"For the pediatrician, psychoanalytic reflection gives meaning to the facts of psychosomatic observations and avoids subjecting them to sterile phenomenological catalogs; for the psychoanalyst, the pediatrician's observation can avoid deviations, chronological errors resulting from a mythical baby reconstituted by the prediction of the past"* (Kreisler, 1999, p.314).

The medical view provides the symptoms for a given illness and psychosomatic knowledge integrates the relational and the mental. It's important to take into account the age of the child, as pathology carries its mark on both biological and mental development.

A child's psychosomatic development takes place progressively, from primitive functioning (dependence on the mother) to the construction of autonomous defenses (end of the second year). In order to assess the baby's psychosomatic economy, it is important to take into account their interactions, mother-child (or someone who looks after the baby), called real interaction, fantastical interaction (these are the unconscious-conscious dimensions); development (psychosomatic in the personality and those of the representative functions, such as in the perceptual-motor system, the functioning of the pre-conscious, etc.); and behavior (analysis of the psychosomatic functioning).); and behavior (analysis of the child's behavior, which is very important, especially when the child doesn't speak; in the child's relationship with others).

The somatic responses presented vary from child to child, as they depend on each one's own dispositions, as well as on whether they are innate or acquired through primary experiences. *"The differences stem from the genetic equipment, the conditions of intrauterine life, in both its biological and psychological data, the conditions of birth and the physical and environmental circumstances that follow"* (Kreisler, 1999, p.361). This shows that no two babies are the same and that this individuality interferes with possible later psychosomatic development.

The illness brings traumatic events that mark the child's life. Illness causes aggression, both internal and external. The body becomes a place of suffering, submissive to external events.

The first months of life are the gestational period for the psyche. The illnesses of an early relationship can be extremely damaging, both for the embryo's body, which suffers the aggressions of intrauterine life, and for the psyche.

Considering that motherhood is the fruit of a woman's last phase of psychological maturation, the birth of a sick child can give the mother a feeling of incapacity, of not trusting herself. The child's father appears dejected and resigned to his son's illness, in contrast to the mother who fights a battle, showing herself to be lucid at all times, sensitive to the life she has given birth to.

According to Mannoni (1988, p. 02):

The mother-child love relationship will always have a residue of denied death, disguised most of the time in sublime love, sometimes in pathological indifference, sometimes in conscious refusal; but the ideas of murder exist, even if not all mothers are aware of it.

This is linked to a desire to commit suicide because of the condemnation of the child, and the mother may feel as if the child is her own condemnation. When pregnancy arrives, the woman can place the task of filling in what was left in the past on her child, creating a phantasmatic image of the baby. When the child is born, she is faced with illness, which can prevent her from resolving her Oedipus complex, because this arrival at femininity will mean that she will have to renounce her imaginary child.

The child is, at first, an evocation of the mother's childhood, which has been lost. She raises her unborn child with a memory that includes wounds suffered, which are expressed in a language of the body or the heart. When the child is born, it brings the first disappointment of now being made of flesh, not as she imagined, and being separated from her. The symptom often exposes the mother's anguish.

The mother's assessment is indispensable when investigating a child's psychosomatic illness. Attention should be paid to the psychological phenomena linked to the birth, which may be the result of an initial relationship, already intrauterine.

As an adaptation to the mother's responses, the child's physiological needs lie in the lack of adaptation to this illness. The child is not only interested in the mother's libidinal investments in the body, but in the body as a whole.

For children, the body is the environment in which they can expose their discomfort. The choice of the diseased organ can be linked to the young child's ability to put into action defense mechanisms adapted to the situation, which is a deviation from further adaptation.

4. Psycho-oncology and childhood cancer

In the Middle Ages, there was a separation between body and mind, and illnesses were considered divine punishment. This dualistic view gave rise to what is now called the biomedical model, which proposes that illnesses can be explained by a biochemical imbalance and have no connection with psychological or social aspects.

However, at the end of the 19th century, Freud, based on mind-body integration, demonstrated that psychic events can influence the organic. From these studies by Freud and other scholars, the field of research and practice of Psychosomatic Medicine began to emerge.

In 1970, an area of psychology called health psychology emerged, which aimed to work with the promotion and maintenance of health, the prevention and treatment of illnesses, the identification of etiology and diagnosis and action in the social health policy system. In the field of oncology, psychologists only began to be in demand in the 70s. The first studies with psychological variables were carried out in the 50s. More significant advances in psycho-oncology were made in the 80s.

Pediatric oncology is an area of medicine that specializes in the study of childhood cancer. Pediatric psycho-oncology is a relatively new segment of psychology, which is located in the field of health psychology and studies the influence of psychological aspects on the manifestation of childhood cancer.

Cancer is a disease characterized by cell mutations and uncontrolled proliferation. For the disease to appear, a number of factors must operate: genetic predisposition, exposure to environmental risk factors, the use of cigarettes, alcohol and illicit drugs, etc. Psychological factors are also believed to influence the onset of cancer (Carvalho, 2002).

An organism is capable of recognizing its components, such as the ego, to allow harmony in the experience of different cell populations. However, at any time, it may not recognize a part of the ego, thus considering it the non-ego and creating antibodies to fight it (Schavelzon, 1999).

The antibodies exist because of the knowledge of the ego, in order to then recognize the non-ego. The liver, pancreas, kidneys, etc. are then fought, and this behavior is known as self-aggression. In this way, we see the problem of the appearance of cancer as a modification that occurs completely in the organism and not just as an aggressive invasion (Schavelzon, 1999).

This reading of the non-ego can be understood as an adaptive response of the individual's organism to a level of stress. It is the organism's response combined with the person's life history.

The diagnosis of cancer brings with it a series of impasses. There's the imminent proximity of death, all the reactions he may have due to the effects of the treatment, such as hair loss, changes in physical appearance, etc. There are also organ damage caused by the drugs, which are very strong.

In addition, there is the experience of mourning these losses. The patient has to deal with all these events, which are very painful, with the uncertainty of what might happen, the fear of recurrence or metastasis. On top of all this, there is fear, pain and suffering in the face of the disease and treatment.

The patient's grief must always be respected, but care must be taken when it is accompanied by deep depression. The improvement of this condition is evident through a resumption and realization of affection. All of the patient's reactions, as well as the duration of their responses, vary according to their personality structure. However, the patient's family, social environment, doctor and other social factors also influence his behavior.

Cancer in children most often affects cells in the blood system, while cancer in adults affects cells in the epithelium. Malignant diseases in children are predominantly embryonic, which is why early diagnosis is so important.[1]

In the United States, childhood cancer is the second leading cause of death among children and adolescents under the age of 15. Since 1970, there has been a linear increase in the cure rates for childhood tumors. In Brazil, Acute Lymphatic Leukemia tumors are cured in around 70% to 80% of cases. However, there has been an increase in the incidence rates of tumors in children, especially ALL. Progress in treating children with cancer has been spectacular over the last four decades. Around 70% of affected children, if diagnosed early and treated in specialized centers, can be cured.[2]

The treatments used for children with cancer are the same as for adults:

chemotherapy, radiotherapy and surgery. These treatments are applied individually for each type of tumor and according to the extent of the disease.

Cancer is rare in childhood and its onset is more associated with genetic factors. There is a high rate of retiniblastoma; lymphoid leukemia and brain tumors are among the most frequent groups of tumors, and Acute Lymphatic Leukemia is among the five causes of cancer death.

Work carried out in the field of psycho-oncology reports the importance of studying two psychological dimensions present in cancer patients: the impact of cancer on the emotional functioning of the patient, their family and the health professionals involved in their treatment; and the role of psychological and behavioral variables in cancer incidence and survival.

Psychological work, be it support, counseling, rehabilitation or individual and group psychotherapy, has facilitated the transmission of the diagnosis, the acceptance of treatment, the relief of side effects, the achievement of a better quality of life and, in terminally ill patients, a better quality of death and dying (Carvalho, 2002).

People who follow the biomedical model repudiate any attempt to link the psychosomatic with the onset of cancer. The work of psychologists is often not recognized by doctors, but there are already hospitals where psychologists are valued and requested by both the medical and nursing staff.

Interview report

1st Interview - D.

D.P.O.C., 10 years old, is the youngest child of a couple who have two other children. She has Acute Myeloid Leukemia, a malignant disease in which chromosomal translocations are present, which lead to the fusion of parts of the genes involved, coding for altered proteins that disrupt cellular signals. This type of leukemia is more common in individuals over the age of thirty, while the incidence in children is less than 15%. He arrived at the institution on April 15, 2004; he is currently undergoing chemotherapy and waiting for a bone marrow transplant.

Talking to D.'s mother, she says that her daughter is a very intelligent, cheerful and very special girl. She doesn't show any sadness, she doesn't seem to think anything of her illness, she wants to study, she likes to get up early because she doesn't want to waste time, she wants to take part in everything.

The child's pregnancy went without a hitch, and all the necessary tests were carried out before the birth. The pregnancy wasn't wanted, but it went very smoothly, bringing a lot of joy. D. was born weighing four kilos and four hundred grams and was a very smart baby.

The girl is always surrounded by friends, makes friends easily and is never alone. At school she's a good student, only having difficulty with math.

One day, D. wasn't the first to get up at home as usual, she felt a lot of pain in her legs, and for this reason she didn't go to school for two days, later the pain moved to her arms, she went to the doctor, who prescribed a pain medication, relieving the symptoms temporarily, then the pain in her legs returned, so she went to the orthopedist, underwent several tests and her ontological illness was discovered, and she was referred to an oncologist. Everyone cried at the news.

In April, a friend of her father's recommended that they come to Sao Paulo. Her mother was worried about the cost, as they had no money, but her father encouraged her and her daughter to come.

When they arrived, D. thought she would only stay a short time, but then her mother revealed that she had leukemia and that they would be spending a long time together. The patient's mother believes that her daughter doesn't think anything about the disease, but she sees her friends dying and thinks that's why she knows about it.

At the hospital, she doesn't give the doctors and nurses any trouble, she knows that she has to undergo tests because of her medical condition, and she does them quite calmly. She's only sad when she's in hospital.

Today he is undergoing oral chemotherapy, while waiting for the bone marrow transplant, to stabilize the condition, which was under control, and suddenly came back much stronger. The child had a very bad time during the first chemotherapy. Even today, when this treatment is very strong, she sometimes gets a fever and feels nauseous for a day or two.

She really likes this house, she just doesn't want to stay in hospital.

There are days when they feel sad about being away from their family, and when D. sees her mother thinking, she asks her not to think, "that she has to be happy" (sic). The girl is very affectionate and very jealous of her mother, they are very close, they talk a lot about everything, she even talks about her flings. Her mother feels that her daughter likes her father a lot, but believes that he likes her more.

2nd Interview - L.

L.G.A. is 8 years old, the eldest daughter of a couple who have another daughter. She has Retinoblastoma, which is a malignant intraocular tumor that is common in childhood. It originates from embryonic neural cëШC of the retina and is transmitted by the autosomal dominant model, although it has a recessive genetic etiology. He arrived at the institution on 18/11/1998; he is currently out of treatment, only undergoing follow-up.

The interview was conducted with the mother on August 19, 2005.

L. is a quiet, intelligent, clever girl who is developing normally at the age of eight. Her mother thinks that their relationship is the best it can be, unlike what she believes it is with her other daughter.

The pregnancy was unplanned, her mother was only 16, but she said she felt she had to love and accept the child that was to come. All the necessary tests were carried out, she felt quite nauseous, but even in her belly, the child was calm.

The child's father said that he wasn't the father, and her mother said that when L. was big and beautiful, she wouldn't be his daughter either; she thinks that the girl has her father's physiognomy, she's beautiful, but she's calm and, at the same time, explosive like her mother. However, according to information from the institution, the child's mother is not calm, she is very energetic with her daughters.

The child believes that her father is her mother's current partner, as they have been together since L. was a baby. Her mother doesn't have the courage to tell the truth; she intends to do so by the end of this year, encouraged by her husband, believing that her daughter will never stop loving the father who raised her.

The mother doesn't hate the biological father, but she won't take her daughter to him when she turns 18. She thinks that, if she wants to, she will go to him. She says that home is the most important thing there is and that if her husband didn't like the girl, she wouldn't be married to him.

While playing with the little girl, her mother noticed that she had an eye patch. The disease was discovered when L. was four months old. When she was six months old, they came to Sao Paulo and stayed for a whole year. The child was sent for chemotherapy and enucleation. It was very difficult for the mother, who turned eighteen here. She believes that when you live away from the disease, it's absurd. Later you come to see that other people's problems are worse, not that it's good to see your daughter in the worst situation, but it's a learning experience. In the end, the mother didn't accept it, she thinks there should be a test to find out.

At the age of six months, the child had her first surgery and, at eight months, she underwent another surgery and underwent ten months of chemotherapy. The first prosthesis was fitted when L. was only nine months old, in her left eye, which had no chance of recovery. There were six tumors in her right eye, but they were treated with a laser.

L didn't understand anything and as she got older she started asking why her mother didn't have a prosthesis, putting her finger in her eye. It was at the age of 4 that she received an explanation about the disease. On one occasion, a boy asked her why she had a crooked eye. She replied that she wore a prosthesis and was undergoing treatment in Sao Paulo.

The girl is monitored every six months. Over the past seven years, the lesion hasn't progressed, but this year her eyesight is getting worse. Her mother sometimes thinks that if the disease comes back, it will be more difficult.

The child is attached to his mother. Her mother says she doesn't differentiate between her children and doesn't give her any privileges because she has problems, so if she has to fight, her mother fights. There are many fights with her sister because she's very messy. L. relates easily to the children, plays, talks to everyone and goes everywhere.

He's in second grade, he always gets ten marks, he does everything, "he's a normal child, he doesn't have any problems" (sic); diverging from the opinion of the teacher who thinks that a problem can incapacitate a student.

3rd Interview - Y.

Y.T.N.V, 10 years old, is the youngest child of a couple who have three children, two girls and a boy. She has Retinoblastoma, which is a malignant intraocular tumor that is common in childhood. It originates from embryonic neural cёCкз of the retina and is transmitted by the autosomal dominant model, although it has a recessive genetic etiology. He arrived at the institution on 01/01/1996; he is currently out of treatment, only undergoing follow-up.

The interview was conducted with the mother on August 26, 2005.

Y. is a very cheerful girl who laughs all the time and only gets upset when someone talks about her deformity. Otherwise, she never complains about anything and is always talking.

Her pregnancy was a bit complicated for her mother, as she didn't accept it. She was depressed at first, but never tried to abort. The family's life was difficult financially and her mother was unemployed, so she got a job and had to hide her belly to keep working. She felt very sick for the first three months and the baby started to move early, before she was two months pregnant, having had all the necessary tests before the baby was born. In the last month, the pregnancy began to be accepted by the mother.

After the child was born, he received all his mother's love, even more than her other children. The two got on well, and are very close today.

When the mother went to feed the baby for the first time, she noticed all the details of the baby and saw that there was a small spot in its eye, which she could only see. Only later, when the child got older, did people start to notice it. She went to the pediatrician because, in addition to the eye patch, the left side of her face was always red. At one year and three months, when they came to Sao Paulo, L's eye was already bigger and looked like a lemon.

They had no support from anyone in the family, only the child's grandmother. The parents don't get along, he isn't present in Y.'s life, but they live in the same house.

Her grandmother was the one who took the child for the first time, and she thought it would be a quick treatment. As it wasn't, Y.'s mother came so that her grandmother could go home.

When the patient's mother heard the doctor say that he had no explanation for the onset of the disease, she thought her daughter was going to die and put her trust in God's hands.

Staying in the house is sad for the mother, because she is in a house that is not hers, but where she finds support from people who are going through similar situations.

When Y. was three years old, she asked why she was different, and she continued to ask until last year; her mother explained it in a way that she could understand, but she felt that her daughter didn't understand because she didn't have a reason for the appearance of the illness. Her mother thought it might be because she'd had four ultrasounds, but this wasn't true.

The girl gets on well with her siblings, sometimes, but they feel jealous, believing that their mother is neglecting them and giving preference to Y.

Y.has been in care for nine years and out of treatment for seven. Today she misses her home when she goes away, but when she was younger she didn't smile, she didn't radiate life like she does now. If she feels sad, she doesn't show it, it stays inside her.

She does very well at school and has no difficulty with any subject. Sometimes she feels ashamed of her deformity, the children talk about it, and she always explains about her oncological illness.

Her mother feels sad, she thinks about the girl's future, whether she will find someone who wants to be with her, whether it will be difficult for her daughter to think that she could be rejected by a boy; but the patient doesn't think ahead, she only asks about her past, and her mother doesn't show her feelings about her daughter's future.

The girl helps her mother overcome her sadness by the way she is, likes to be busy all the time, and never watches TV.

<u>Observing the children</u>

Group activity

On October 19, an observation was made of the children during their participation in the Corelim Group. The Group is a psycho-oncological program for children and adolescents with cancer, which aims to mobilize and strengthen the children's internal resources during the process of treatment and recovery from the disease.

The group worked as follows: first, the children introduced themselves, then they were given some cards with drawings of dolls with different expressions, so that they could pick the one that most resembled what they were feeling and explain why they had chosen it, then they listened to a story, drew about it and, finally, in a circle with everyone holding hands, they said the part of the story that they liked the most and, in a chorus, the children repeated it. All the group activities were carried out with the children on the floor and barefoot.

D., an attentive girl, who looked after her handicapped classmate all the time: she cuddled her, talked to her, held hands with her. L. interacts with her friends, but always around the monitors, asking for approval. Y., an independent girl, a soft child, very observant.

- I'm L., I'm eight years old and I've come for an eye exam.
- I'm D., I live in Paraguay and I came here to have a leukemia transplant; I'm in the queue.
- No, it's me! My name is Y., I'm 10 years old now, I...I came to the house ....I'm Y., I'm 10 years old and I just came to the house to get my ears checked.

- Y. (chose the blank card) C I chose it because I don't know, I'm more or less happy, because the pencil murderer pierced my hand.
- D. C I chose this letter, the 23rd, because I'm wondering what's going to happen, if

it's going to turn into a mess or if it already has.

- Monitors C In the group?

- D. C E.

- L. C I chose this letter because I'm ashamed.

- Monitoras C Why, are you ashamed of someone?

- L C No.

The story told to the children was as follows:

In an ancient Persian kingdom, a very beautiful kingdom, there was a boy named Samuel. He was in the street and saw a princess passing by in a procession, but in this country it was forbidden to see the princess's face. He saw the princess's face as she drove by in the procession, and Samuel fell from the tree and was arrested. One day, a man came to the prison and offered to help him out of jail, his name was Jafar. It was night, he stole the key from the guard who was asleep, they walked through the desert and found a secret passage.

Jafar then told Samuel what he wanted: - I want you to go through a tunnel, enter the palace, go to the end of it and take a lamp. Samuel thought it was strange, but he went. He tripped on a ladder and when he opened his eyes he was in the castle garden and found the lamp, only when he picked it up there was a violent earthquake. He managed to get out and when he reached the tunnel he met Jafar, who said give me the lamp and I'll pull you out. Samuel didn't want to give it to him, but when the earthquake hit, he fell into the tunnel and Jafar took the lamp. Samuel managed to get out and went after Jafar because he was evil.

Jafar had already made two requests, which were: first to be very rich and powerful, and he became very rich and powerful, and the second was to marry Princess Samira, but the genie said he couldn't change her feelings, so Jafar said he wanted to get married, whether she liked it or not. So he married the princess, but the princess wasn't happy and Jafar was doing evil.

Knowing this story, Samuel started a sword fight with Jafar, al Samuel was wounded, and remembered that Jafar had not made the third request, so Samuel told Jafar that he was not the most powerful man, because the most powerful man was the genie, then Jafar asked to be more powerful than the genie. The genie then became human and Jafar became the genie, returning to the lamp.

Samuel and Princess Samira get the lamp and take it to the sultan, the princess's father. Samuel asks the princess for her hand in marriage, her father gives it and they rebuild the city, get married and Samuel becomes a sultan.

Throughout the story, D. kept quiet and paid attention, she was sitting on the floor next to her disabled classmate, she got up and sat on the sofa, taking a teddy bear for herself and putting one next to her friend. Try to get the other children to be quiet.

L. sits next to the monitors, holding hands, for a moment.

Y. interacts with other children, doesn't sit still for long. She's the most talkative.

When, at the end of the story, the children are asked what to do with the lamp, D. replies that she would throw it in the river. The monitor then asks: - What if it floated away?

- D. C was going to stay in a place far from Baghdad, on the sea.

L. talks to the monitor about the story, saying that she would melt the lamp and make a piece of jewelry.

D., always the quietest, asks the monitors for the drawing board to draw the end of the story. Y. sits down next to D. and they start to draw. Y. draws on the front of the sheet, then draws on the back, crumples up the sheet, says she made a mistake and asks for a new sheet to draw another picture. She asks the monitors for water, always politely, asking please.

D., next to Y., is annoyed by the noise she is making with her pencil and asks her friend to stop. L, always together with one of the monitors, asks for help to point the pencil, showing her drawing to see if they like it. She hands over the drawing she's finished and asks for another sheet of paper, makes a heart and a flower with the monitor's name on it, hands her the drawing and gets a hug.

Y. then asks what we're writing down, why we're holding the drawing sheet she's crumpled up in her hand, I say nothing and offer her the drawing back, she then says she doesn't want it and that we can keep it. As she interacts with her classmates, she laughs forgivingly.

D. shows her drawing, but says she hasn't finished it yet. L. then asks our name.

When all the children had finished their drawings, a circle was formed and, with everyone holding hands, including us, they said, one by one, the part we liked best in the story, so that the rest could repeat it in chorus.

D. said it was the part where Samuel married Samira.

Y. that Samuel is brave.

L., joking as he spoke, recounted the part that Samuel won.

At the end, all the criangas greeted the people watching the group and left. They clearly enjoyed the activity and all went away very happy.

Process Analysis

We selected three girls, aged between 8 and 10, who had an oncological illness. The information we gathered about these children was by observing their interaction in groups and by interviewing their mothers.

D. is a very serene girl, concerned about the people around her and always very helpful. She has Acute Myeloid Leukemia, is currently undergoing chemotherapy and is in line for a bone marrow transplant. L is the youngest of the three girls. She is very clever and shows that she needs the approval of the people around her. She has retinoblastoma and has had her left eye enucleated, chemotherapy and laser treatments. Nowadays, she is monitored every six months. Y. is a very smiley and communicative girl who also has retinoblastoma. She has had her left eye enucleated and has had chemotherapy, laser and radiotherapy treatments. She is only being monitored by her doctor.

By correlating the cases observed with the data obtained, we were able to find a number of similarities that are relevant to our study. These include: the unwanted pregnancy, the mother's relationship with the child, the stage of psychic development the child is in, the denial of the mother, the question of femininity x motherhood, the daughter put in the place of mother, the way of coping with illness and mourning.

The mother's relationship with the child suggests that the oncological disease arose from an unwanted pregnancy, full of hurt and resentment. As an example, Y.'s mother reports that: "the pregnancy was a bit complicated because I didn't accept it, but I never tried to abort it" (sic), for L.'s mother "the pregnancy wasn't planned because I was only 16" (sic) and, D.'s mother says that "the pregnancy wasn't wanted, but it was quite peaceful" (sic). The disturbances of childhood, then, are failures in the mother's first relationships with her baby, which releases excess excitement into the somatic, because it doesn't have psychic autonomy. These symptoms appear in the body, making it a source of expression.

These are the first months of life, the gestational period of the psyche, and the ailments of the initial relationship with the mother can be harmful, both to the embryo's body, which will suffer the aggressions of later life, and to its psyche. This situation is evident when Y.'s mother tells of having hidden her belly in the first months of pregnancy in order to continue working.

When D. sees her mother sad, she asks her not to think, because she has to be happy. It is the little girl who supports her mother, who helps her to cope with difficulties. The appearance of the disease in the bone marrow is relevant, as it is an organ that supports the body. The choice of the diseased organ may be due to the child's ability to activate defense mechanisms adapted to the situation.

The mother doesn't show her suffering, her anguish. She doesn't talk about the pain of having a sick child, she insists that everything is fine; the birth of a sick child can cause the mother to feel incapable, of not trusting herself. She uses the mechanism of denial, which is a coping mechanism, to avoid fear, suffering and despair in the face of events. L.'s mother says that her daughter is always a grade 10, does everything, "is a normal child and has no problems" (sic). D.'s mother, on the other hand, says: "my daughter is an intelligent, cheerful and special girl" (sic). This also appears in Y.'s mother when she says that her daughter "never complains about anything and is always talking, she's super cheerful and always laughing" (sic).

Neurosis alienates the individual from the reality in which they live. Neurotics distance themselves from reality because they find it unbearable. This process that neurotics go through is known as the primary process and is described as the pleasure-pleasure principle. These processes are based on the effort to achieve pleasure; causing the psyche to turn away from activities that generate displeasure. Affective and expressive manifestations were then valued, transformed into action, and provided the process of thinking.

According to Freud (1911, p. 281):

With the introduction of the reality principle, one of the species of thought activity was separated; it was freed from the reality test and remained subordinate only to the pleasure principle. This activity is fantasizing, which began in children's play and was later preserved as daydreaming, abandoning dependence on real objects.

Fantasy is important in the formation of symptoms, because it protects from reality, reduces feelings of guilt or other feelings, because there is no certainty of the facts (as in the case of a crime, for example).

Being a mother affects a woman's femininity and when a child is ill, this issue comes to the fore; it's not the difficulty of motherhood, but the acceptance of women as female subjects. This behavior is clear when D.'s mother expresses sadness at being away from her family, when Y.'s mother is sad at being in a house that isn't hers and when L.'s mother doesn't accept her daughter's illness at first.

When we learn about D.'s life story, in which the girl takes on the role of mother, always supporting her, even in relation to her oncological illness; the girl presents with leukemia, which is a type of cancer that affects the bone marrow, which is an organ that sustains the body, explaining the relationship she has with her mother.

We experienced two other very similar stories. L. and Y. both had the same type of cancer, retinoblastoma, which is a genetic disease, and their history includes the fact that their mothers didn't want them to be pregnant. L.'s mother became pregnant at the age of 16 without planning it, while Y.'s mother says she didn't accept her pregnancy and became depressed at first.

The daughter is the one who supports her mother's suffering, who makes up for her sadness with her way of facing her illness. She faces an oncological illness and expresses it in a world of colors, laughter, full of jokes, radiating life and strength to the people around her. According to L.'s mother, her daughter "relates easily to children, plays, talks to everyone and goes everywhere" (sic). Y.'s mother says that "I overcome my sadness because of the way she is, she likes to always be busy and watch TV" (sic), "if she gets sad she doesn't show it, she stays inside" (sic) and D.'s mother says that her daughter "doesn't show her sadness, she doesn't seem to think anything about her illness, she wants to study, she likes to get up early because she doesn't want to waste time, she wants to take part in everything" (sic).

In the face of all this, along with the illness comes the imminent risk of the child's death, which contradicts the natural cycle of life; melancholy at the difficulty of the facts and mourning itself. According to Y.'s mother, "when I heard the doctor say that there was no explanation for the onset of the illness, I thought my daughter was going to die and I put it in God's hands" (sic).

Mourning is the reaction to the loss of someone, of a loved one, but there are people who, in the same situation, produce melancholy; they are suspected of having some pathology. For Freud (1916 [1915]), mourning is a normal attitude, which is overcome over time and medical help is dispensed with.

The characteristics that identify melancholy are: extremely painful despondency, loss of interest in the outside world, cessation of the ability to love, a drop in self-esteem that finds expression in self-recrimination and self-blame, and even an expectation of punishment, complemented by insomnia and refusal to eat. It is essential from a therapeutic point of view to contradict what the patient says against his own ego. These same traits are found in bereavement, except for the disturbance in self-esteem.

In mourning, it is revealed that the beloved object no longer exists, and it is important to withdraw libido from this connection. Memories are evoked and libido is withdrawn from each one. When the task of mourning is finally finished, the ego is free again.

In melancholia, you only know the meaning of who you've lost, but not what you've lost in that something. The free libido, instead of finding another object, shifts to the ego, which can be judged as the abandoned object.

According to Freud (1916 [1915]), in melancholia, the occasions that give rise to the illness go, for the most part, beyond the clear case of a loss by death, including situations of disregard, contempt or disappointment, which can bring into the relationship opposing feelings of love and hate or reinforce an already existing ambivalence. This ambivalence is shown to exist by real experiences, or by constitutional factors, and should be considered as preconditions for the existence of melancholy. In mourning it's the external world that becomes poor, in melancholia it's the ego, but both disappear without leaving any major changes.

Based on the facts collected, we saw similarities in the mothers' behavior towards their daughters. Their speeches illustrate the denial of the illness, the suffering and the disappointment in the face of the illness is expressed by the mothers' sadness. Because they attribute the illness to chance, they believe that if their daughters became ill it was because God wanted them to, thus absolving themselves of blame.

When mothers learn of the diagnosis of a chronic and fatal illness, they sometimes seek refuge in denial of their child's illness, building a barrier between their fantasy (idealized child) and reality (sick child).

The mourning of the idealized son, the bearer of all perfection, needs to be dealt with so that the mother doesn't become paralyzed in her narcissistic wound and starts to help her daughter build her own narcissism, her body image and can see more than a sick son.

<u>Conclusion</u>

The complexity of the mother-daughter relationship leads to the emergence of an ambiguous relationship between them, one of love and hate. The girl desires her father and feels jealous of her mother for possessing him, as well as blaming her for his castration.

The development of psychosomatic illness is anchored in children's primitive relationships with others and they discharge the excitement they are subjected to into the somatic because they do not yet have psychic autonomy. Symptoms can arise because of the absence of words and children can express themselves through somatic illness. The choice of the diseased organ is related to the complex situation in which the girl is involved.

We have seen in the cases explained that, rather than an event in the child's body, somatic illness is a fact of discourse, which is linked to the place that the child occupies in the parental fantasy. The mother creates a phantasmatic image of the baby and, when it is born, she is faced with the characteristics of that child, which were not desired. The image of the real baby generates anguish in the mother, a feeling that is transferred to the child, who can express it through the somatic. The child can use the illness as a means of expression, because they feel closed off from the truth.

In the cases analyzed, we found stories of unwanted pregnancies, with difficulties in maternal acceptance. The mother's feelings seem to be transmitted to the child, who may then hide in the illness, waiting for a real word from the mother.

When the mother is faced with her daughter's illness, she may use the mechanism of denial to protect herself from reality. It is important that she mourns the idealized child in order to come to terms with the reality in which she finds herself. Facing her daughter as she is, she can see more than a sick child, helping her to build her narcissism.

Another factor that draws attention is the question of femininity. When faced with a sick child, the woman fixates on her maternal role, forgetting about her other roles. She devotes all her energy to this child, leaving aside her husband, her other children and her life in society. She gives up her life to look after her daughter, as a way of minimizing her guilt.

The imminent risk of death, due to her daughter's fatal illness, runs counter to the natural cycle of life, creating a feeling of helplessness in the mother. The difficulty of dealing with this situation causes the woman to mourn. At this point, her daughter plays an extremely important role: by facing the illness in a softer way, with more energy and overflowing with life, she brings her mother into her reality and tries to ease her suffering.

It is important for children to know what their mothers are feeling, because through this they can attribute meaning to what they are experiencing. In the child's speech, there is concern for the mother.

Psycho-oncology can appear as a somatic illness, in which the animal expresses itself in the physical. The children with somatic illnesses with whom we have had contact are very active in therapeutic groups and, through play, they express the feelings they are experiencing and the difficulties they are facing, using play to symbolize the anguish related to the moment they are going through. We can think that, as Freud (1920) states, children find in play a way of expressing their displeasure. For him, play is not opposed to what is serious, but to what is real, and children use play to deal with reality. They don't make jokes like adults, but they seek the pleasure principle in order to deal with the suffering caused by reality.

Children face the illness in a plausible way, they don't seem to be aware that they are suffering from a fatal chronic illness. We know, however, that the symptom is evident because it is a display of the unconscious suffering that accompanies them throughout their lives.

In the mothers' speeches, when we didn't refer to the disease, they told a story of a daughter without illnesses, who was developing normally; denying the disease as a way of defending themselves from the pain caused by the image of their sick daughter.

Through this research, we were able to understand the mother-daughter relationship in psychosomatic illness. We hope to be able to enhance the field of psycho-oncology by contributing to future studies.

Bibliographical references

CRUZ, Anamaria da Costa. **Presenting academic work:** guides for students at Mackenzie Presbyterian University. 2.ed. Sao Paulo: Editora Mackenzie, 2003.

CARVALHO, Maria Margarida. **Psycho-oncology:** History, characteristics and challenges. [Scientific article]. 2002. Available at: http://www.scielo.com.br. Accessed on: 18 Dec. 04.

COSTA JUNIOR, A.L. **Psycho-Oncology and management of invasive procedures in pediatric oncology:** a literature review. [Scientific article]. 1999. Available at: http://www.scielo.com.br. Accessed on: October 24, 05.

DJOURS.C. Biology, psychoanalysis and somatization. In: VOLICH, M.R.; FERRAZ, F.C.; ARANTES, M.A.A.C. **Psicossoma II:** Psicossomatica psicanalitica. Sao Paulo: Casa do psicologo, 1998. p. 17-31.

EKSTERMAN, A. Psicossomatica: o diálogo entre a psicanalise e a medicina. In: MELLO FILHO, J. **PsicossomaticaHoje.** Sao Paulo: Artmed, 1992. p. 77-88.

EPIDEMOLOGY of tumors in children and adolescents. Ministry of Health: National Cancer Institute . Available at: http://www.inca.gov.br. Accessed on: 6 Mar. 05.

GRUNSPUN, H. Psychosomatic symptoms and psychosomatic disorders in children. In: **Psychosomatic disorders in children:** The crying body. Sao Paulo: Atheneu, 1978. p. 1-17.

GRUNSPUN, H. Developmental theories of psychosomatic disorders in children. In: **Psychosomatic disorders in children:** The crying body. Sao Paulo: Atheneu, 1978. p.19-47.

GRUNSPUN, H. Diagnosis of psychosomatic disorders in children. In: **Psychosomatic disorders in children:** The crying body. Sao Paulo: Atheneu, 1978. p.49-85.

FREUD, S. About transience (1916 [1915]). In: *Obras Completas*. v. XIV. Rio de Janeiro: Imago, 1996. p.345-350...

FREUD, S. The psychoanalytic conception of the psychogenic disturbance of vision (1910). In: *Complete Works*. Rio de Janeiro: Imago, 1996. p.197-206.

FREUD, S. The dissolution of the Oedipus complex (1924). In: *Obras Completas*. v. XIX. Rio de Janeiro: Imago, 1996. p. 215-226.

FREUD, S. Some psychic consequences of the anatomical distinction between the sexes (1925). In: *Obras Completas*. v. XIX. Rio de Janeiro: Imago, 1996. p. 303-322.

FREUD, S. The infantile genital organization (1923). In: *Obras Completas*. v. XIX. Rio de Janeiro: Imago, 1996. p. 177-186.

FREUD, S. Aldm of the pleasure principle (1920). In: *Complete Works*. Rio de Janeiro: Imago, 1996. p. 17-90.

FREUD, S. Lecture XXXIV: Explanations, applications and orientations (1933 [1934]). In: *Obras Completas*. v. XXII. Rio de Janeiro: Imago, 1996. p. 167-192.

FREUD, S. Femininity (1932). In: *Complete Works*. Rio de Janeiro: Imago, 1996. p.139-166.

FREUD, S. Formulation on the two principles of mental functioning (1911). In: *Obras Completas*. v. XII. Rio de Janeiro: Imago, 1996. p.273-286.

FREUD, S. Mourning and melancholia (1916 [1915]). In: *Obras Completas*. v. XIV. Rio de Janeiro: Imago, 1996. p. 271-292.

FREUD, S. Creative writers and their daydreams (1908 [1907]). In: *Complete Works*. V. IX. Rio de Janeiro: Imago, 1996. p. 149-158.

FREUD, S. The meaning of symptoms (1917 [1916]). In: *Complete Works.* V. XVI. Rio de Janeiro: Imago, 1996. p. 305 - 322.

FREUD, S. Romance familiares (1909 [1908]). In: *Obras Completas.* v. IX. Rio de Janeiro: Imago, 1996. p.243-247.

FREUD, S. Female sexuality (1932). In: *Complete Works.* Rio de Janeiro: Imago, 1996. p. 259-282.

FREUD, S. On the sexual theories of the child (1908). In: *Obras Completas.* v. IX. Rio de Janeiro: Imago, 1996. p. 209-228.

FREUD, S. On narcissism: an introduction (1914). In: *Complete Works.* v. XIV. Rio de Janeiro: Imago, 1996. p. 89-122.

FREUD, S. Dream and occultism (1933 [1932]). In: *Obras Completas.* v. XXII. Rio de Janeiro: Imago, 1996. p. 45-74.

FREUD, S. Animistic treatment (1905). In: *Obras Completas.* v. VII. Rio de Janeiro: Imago, 1996. p. 266-285.

HOLANDA, S.A.R. Premature babies in the I.T.U.: Motherhood in question. In: *Estilos de clinica:* Revista sobre a infancia com problemas. V.1, n.1. Sao Paulo: USP-IP, 1996. p. 5869.

KREISLER, Lëon. Somatic expression in infant psychopathology. In: *The new child of psychosomatic disorder.* Sao Paulo: Casa do psicologo, 1999. p 313-320.

KREISLER, Lëon. The psychosomatic pathology of the abandoned, abused and severely disorganized child. In: *The new child of psychosomatic disorder.* Sao Paulo: Casa do psicologo, 1999. p 199-208.

KREISLER, Lëon. Notes on psychosomatic equilibrium. Its genesis in the development of the infant. In: *The new child of psychosomatic disorder.* Sao Paulo: Casa do psicologo, 1999. p 348-362.

KREISLER, Lëon. Psychosomatic medicine. In: *The psychosomatic child.* Lisbon: Estampa, 1978. p. 15-19.

KREISLER, Lëon.Various aspects of the psychosomatic clinic of the child. In: *The psychosomatic child*. Lisbon: Estampa, 1978. p. 29-36.

KREISLER, Lëon. The psychosomatic latent. In: *The psychosomatic child.* Lisbon: Estampa, 1978. p. 93-102.

KREISLER, Lëon. Theoretical aspects. In: *The psychosomatic child.* Lisbon: Estampa, 1978. p. 117-129.

MANNONI, Maud. The organic lesion. In: *A crianga retardada e a mae*. 2. ed. Sao Paulo: Martins Fonte. 1998. p. 1- 08.

MANNONI, Maud. The child's phantasmatic relationship with his mother. In: *A crianga retardada e a mae*. 2. ed. Sao Paulo: Martins Fonte. 1998. p. 37-44.

MANNONI, Maud. The place of anxiety in the treatment of the debilitated. In: *A crianga retardada e a mae*. 2. ed. Sao Paulo: Martins Fonte. 1998. p. 45-54.

MANNONI, Maud. Introduction. The psychoanalysis of children based on Freud. In: *The child, his illness and others:* the symptom *and the* word. 3. ed. Rio de Janeiro: Guanabara, 1987. p.09-26.

MANNONI, Maud. The symptom or the word. In: *The child, his illness and others:* the symptom and *the* word. 3. ed. Rio de Janeiro: Guanabara, 1987. p. 29-66

MELLO, A.M. Psychosomatica e pediatria. In: MELLO FILHO, J. *Psicossomatica Hoje*. Sao Paulo: Artmed, 1992. p. 195-207.

NEVES, S.M.R. Brief historical overview of psychoanalytic psychosomatics. In: VOLICH, M.R.; FERRAZ, F.C.; ARANTES, M.A.A.C. *Psicossoma II:* Psicossomatica psicanalitica. Sao Paulo: Casa do psicologo, 1998. p. 35-37.

PARTICULARITIES of childhood cancer. Ministry of Health: National Cancer Institute . Available at: http://www.inca.gov.br. Accessed on: 6 Mar. 05.

PENTEADO, A.F.C. Introduction: Notes on the development of the field of child psychosomatics. In: VOLICH, M.R.; FERRAZ, F.C.; ARANTES, M.A.A.C. *Psicossoma II:* Psicossomatica psicanalitica. Sao Paulo: Casa do psicologo, 1998. p. 117120.

RANNA,W. Pediatrics and psychoanalysis. In: VOLICH, M.R.; FERRAZ, F.C.; ARANTES, M.A.A.C. *Psicossoma II:* Psicossomatica psicanalitica. Sao Paulo: Casa do psicologo, 1998. p. 121-135.

SCHAVELZON, Jose. On psychosomatics and cancer. In: Filho, J.M. *Psicossomatica Hoje*. Sao Paulo: Artmed, 1992. p. 215-226.

VOLICH, M.R. Psychoanalytic foundations of the psychosomatic clinic. In: VOLICH, M.R.; FERRAZ, F.C.; ARANTES, M.A.A.C. *Psicossoma II:* Psicossomatica psicanalitica. Sao Paulo: Casa do psicologo, 1998. p. 17-31.

yes I want morebooks!

Buy your books fast and straightforward online - at one of world's fastest growing online book stores! Environmentally sound due to Print-on-Demand technologies.

Buy your books online at
www.morebooks.shop

Kaufen Sie Ihre Bücher schnell und unkompliziert online – auf einer der am schnellsten wachsenden Buchhandelsplattformen weltweit! Dank Print-On-Demand umwelt- und ressourcenschonend produzi ert.

Bücher schneller online kaufen
www.morebooks.shop

Printed by Books on Demand GmbH, Norderstedt / Germany